Lord Harris Clo

The 5th Lord Harris and his Collection.

A Georgian country house deep in the Kent countryside is perhaps not the obvious home for a clock collection. Until recent years few were aware that at Belmont there is, without doubt, the finest collection of clocks and watches in Britain outside those in the national museums.

The collection was entirely the creation of George St. Vincent, the 5th Baron Harris (of Seringapatam, Mysore and Belmont in the county of Kent to give him his full style). The only child of George Robert Canning and Lucy Ada Jervis (whose ancestor was John Jervis, 1st Earl St.Vincent), George St Vincent went through the usual aristocratic education of the day, schooling at Eton and a degree at Oxford. He served as a Captain in the Kent Yeomanry in the First World War, during which he was wounded and invalided out with the Military Cross for bravery.

After succeeding to the title in 1932, Lord Harris conceived two missions in life, both of which he achieved supremely well. First it fell to him to restore the fortunes of Belmont, which had suffered under the 4th Baron's tendency to 'live life to the full'. By hard and intelligent work on London's

Fig. 1. *The 5th Lord Harris (1889-1984).*

COVER. *Orrery clock by Raingo of Paris c.1830. The orrery mechanism on top revolves once a year and has an annual calendar fitted around it, on top of the clock. (H201)*

S
h   ... the back of
B... ...s double mortgage and put the family seat back onto a sound footing. The second mission he set himself was to create the most representative collection of English clocks in private hands.

He had discovered a passion for horology as a young man in the early years of this century; he tells us, with typical good humoured understatement that he "just liked to see the wheels go round..." At that time Belmont had few clocks of any kind but by the time of his death in 1984, at the grand old age of 95, the house was wholly imbued with the gentle sounds of timekeeping, boasting no less than 340 clocks and watches, most of which he kept working. Lord Harris became deeply involved in the subject too; he served as Master of the Worshipful Company of Clockmakers and was, from 1953, founding President of the Antiquarian Horological Society.

Thanks to the pioneering work of authors like F.J.Britten, R.T.Gould and G.H.Baillie (see *Suggested Reading*), antiquarian horology as a subject was firmly 'on the map' by the late 1920s and there were already one or two well established private collections of clocks, most notably that of D.H.Wetherfield in Blackheath. London dealers such as Percy Webster of Great Portland Street and Clowes and Jauncey of Beauchamp Place began to specialise in selling old clocks and watches to the new breed of horological collector. Indeed, these two companies between them sold Harris over 30% of his entire collection.

1

The Harris collection consists of a wide variety of clocks and watches with examples from all of the major clock making countries and periods. However, clocks from England's horological 'Golden Age', nominally from the mid-seventeenth to the mid-eighteenth centuries, were Harris's first love and many of the clocks at Belmont dating from this period are of national importance.

A contemporary of Harris's, Walter Iden, was also a collector in this field, and when, owing to the bombing of London during the second world war, Iden decided to dispose of the whole collection, Harris was able to acquire several more fine examples for Belmont.

Harris was no armchair collector, he would not only watch "the wheels go round" but would take his clocks to pieces too, carrying out minor repairs and adjustments, though major overhauls were done by professionals, usually from the London firm of Frodsham. His technical interest extended to the collection of clocks with an unusual technical feature or novelty and nearly half of Belmont's clocks could be considered of this kind, a few of them in the form of modern replicas.

Last but by no means least in the Harris collection is a category of clocks and watches from France, all made during the period around the French Revolution, a period when the likes of Abraham Louis Breguet and Antide Janvier made some of the most stylish and elegant designs in horological history. The collection of 27 objects by Breguet (plus 3 'pretenders') is itself one of the most notable in existence.

An aspect of the collection which makes it especially interesting is the presence at Belmont of Lord Harris's meticulously filed letters and documents, a comprehensive record of the process of forming the collection, including suppliers, dates of acquisition and prices paid. As one might expect, the letters make amusing and salutary reading for those interested in the rapid rise in value of antique clocks and watches over the years. There can hardly be a collection of antiques in the world which doesn't include a few 'bad apples' in the barrel and Belmont's is no exception. All collectors have their blind spots, as do most dealers, but it has to be said that in the Harris collection careful study has revealed one or two deliberate forgeries too. The largest of the lantern clocks signed by Joseph Knibb is a rather obvious deception; but one of the four examples signed Thomas Tompion - the hooded wall clock - is extremely convincing and only proved not to be genuine after complete dismantling.

Clocks from the Golden Age.

A chronological look at Belmont's clocks begins in late 16th century Germany with the anonymous tabernacle clock, *Fig. 2*. Throughout the renaissance the greatest centres of the metal working trades in Europe were in South Germany, in cities such as Nuremberg and Augsburg. This was their own horological 'Golden Age' and the tabernacle clock and four other, somewhat later, table clocks represent Germany's contribution well. England's heyday began in the mid seventeenth century, just as Germany's was coming to an end.

In 1657 the great Dutch scientist Christian Huygens invented and patented the first practical pendulum clock, one of the most significant events in all of horological history. Up until then clocks had only been capable of an accuracy of about 15-20 minutes a day and only generally used one hand, an hour hand, to indicate time.

With the pendulum as a controller they could, seemingly overnight, perform to within one minute a day and it became worthwhile fitting clocks with a minute hand. However, it was not in Holland where this new technological wonder had its greatest impact, but in England. London was already growing rapidly into a major centre for clock making, and increasing numbers of craftsmen were setting up in the city and joining the newly formed guild, the Worshipful Company of Clockmakers, which was founded in 1631 as a breakaway company from the Blacksmiths'.

Fig. 2. *Anonymous German gilt-brass tabernacle clock, c.1595. (H211)*

Fig. 3. *Rare, quarter striking lantern clock with hour and minute hands and every minute numbered on the dial, by Davis Mell. The clock was formerly in the Iden Collection. (H107)*

The lantern clock by Davis Mell of London c.1660 (unusually for clocks of this period, quarter striking), is a fine and grand example of the type of clock made in London at this time, *Fig. 3*. The following years were to see clockmakers in that city dominate world horology, many of them Huguenots seeking refuge from persecution abroad and bringing their skills and tastes with them. By 1700, virtually all the features of the modern mechanical clock had been invented and incorporated into clocks made in London. Thus we move straight to the spiritual heart of Lord Harris's collection.

Fig. 4. *Early pendulum clock by Ahasuerus Fromanteel. The historically important movement has been altered, very early in its life, to its present form as a longcase clock. The case is relatively modern but is finely made and in the correct style. (H062)*

It was the Fromanteel family who made the first pendulum clocks in England. On hearing about the new invention, the clockmaker Ahasuerus Fromanteel (1607-1693) sent his son John (1638-c.1682) to Holland to discover its secrets and on 25 November 1658 they advertised in the *Commonwealth Mercury* that they had been "examined and proved before his Highness the Lord Protector".

A very early example of the work of Ahasuerus (and the only one in this collection) is the clock which is now a longcase clock, *Fig. 4*, but which, when first made c.1660, may well have been a wall clock. It would have looked very much like another example in the Harris collection: the wall clock by Edward East (1602-1696) made about 1660, *Plate 1*. The plain columns and simple, but elegant, ebony-veneered architectural-style case of this little clock, make it a first rate example of an early pendulum clock and historically one of the rarest and most important in the collection. Wooden clock cases actually made their first appearance with these new pendulum clocks and they must have seemed very novel, even *avant garde* objects, given their austere styling and the new 'high tech', high accuracy movement.

The reason for the particular rarity of these little wall clocks is connected with the introduction of the longcase clock. The new pendulum wall clocks, which mostly ran for eight days, had much heavier weights, and there is no doubt that the weak plaster walls in 17th century houses would have had difficulty supporting them. The theory is that many must have been destroyed by accidental falls and the logical improvement was to extend the case down to the floor, achieving the additional benefit of protecting the weights from interference (not to protect a long pendulum: long pendulum clocks did not appear until about 10 years later in c.1670). Thus the longcase or 'grandfather' clock was born in the early 1660s and a good example, made in the 1660s by John Fromanteel, is at Belmont. Some wall clocks, the Ahasuerus Fromanteel for example, might have been 'improved' by converting a wall clock case into a longcase.

By the time the longcase clock by Edward East, *Fig. 5*, was completed, c.1675, the longcase was thus firmly established as an

Plate 1. *8 day early pendulum clock by Edward East, London, c.1660. This must rank as one of the earliest English pendulum clocks in existence. (H053)*

4

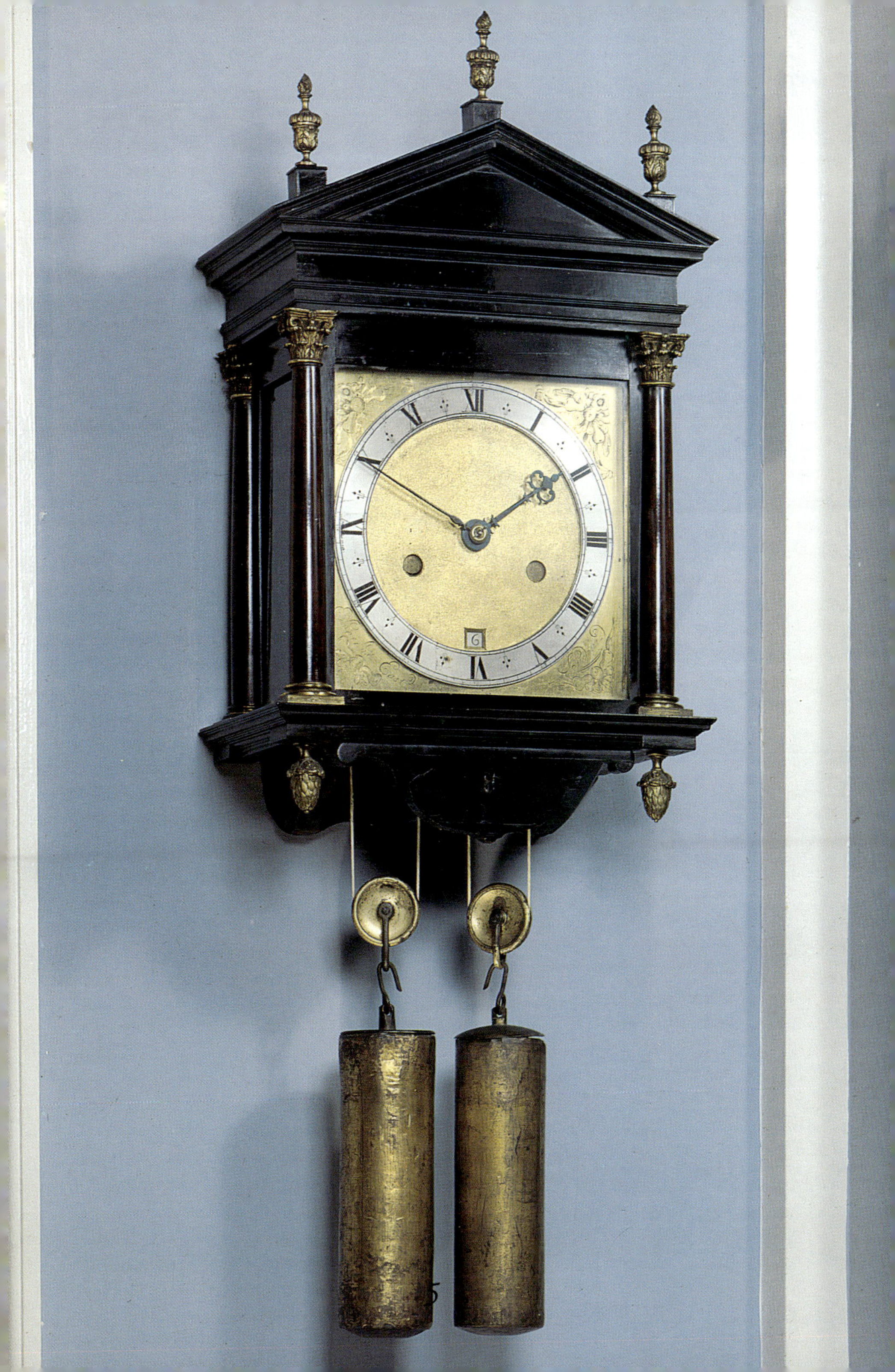

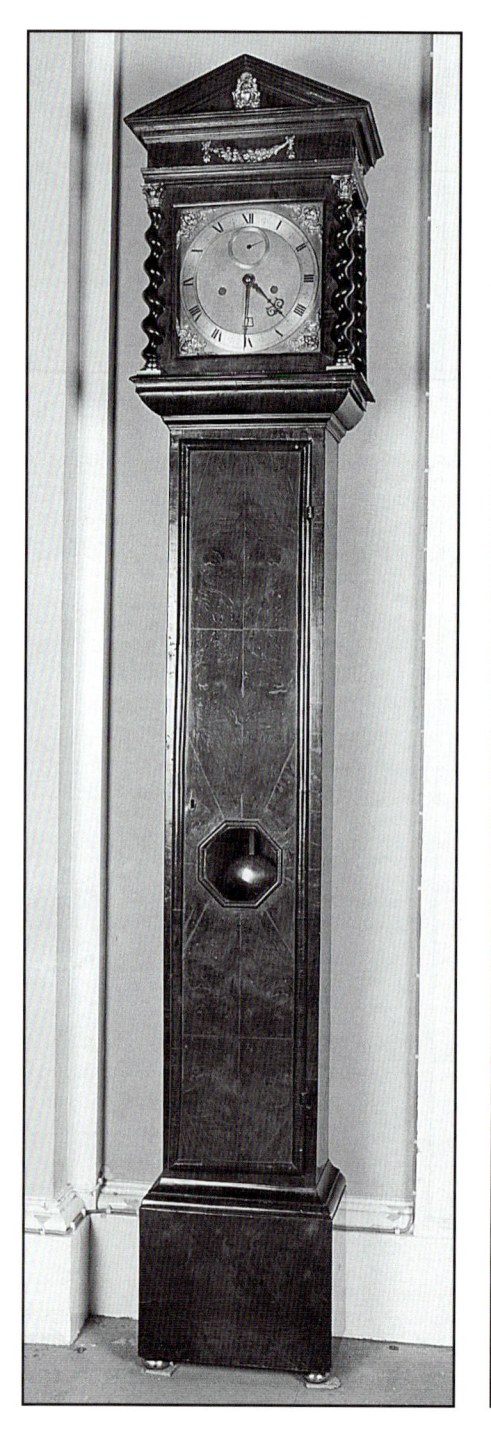

item of household furniture, though high price would have prevented such clocks from appearing in any but the most prosperous of homes. Spring-driven clocks such as the fine table clock by East, *Plate 2*, were particularly expensive, spring clock making being a more difficult and specialised practice.

Another type of spring-driven early pendulum clock which has become particularly rare is the night clock, as in the example by Henry Jones (c.1642-1695) dating c.1670, *Fig. 6*. Jones was one of Edward East's apprentices and East and Jones are the makers most closely associated with this type. The dial has the numbers pierced out, the roman quarters fixed and the arabic hours moving in the semi-circular opening in the dial. At night, a lamp burning on a shelf inside the case illuminates the numbers which can thus be seen from across the darkened room hovering, as it were, in mid air. Needless to say such clocks are now very rare because, in spite of a crude 'chimney' to guide the smoke and heat out of the back of the case, so many must have gone up in flames!

In spite of the Fromanteels' great achievement it was one of the next generation of English clockmakers, Thomas Tompion (1639-1713), who was to be given the title of 'The father of English clockmaking'. Tompion established a finely divided and organised system for watch and clockmaking and, from about 1680, was the first to provide his products with serial numbers. Tompion and his almost exact contemporary Joseph Knibb (1640-1711), the most famous

Fig. 5. *8 day longcase clock with long pendulum and anchor escapement by Edward East, c.1675. An early example of a walnut-veneered case, but retaining the architectural style of the first pendulum clocks. (H055)*

6

Fig. 6. *Night clock by Henry Jones, c.1670. The disc with the arabic hour figures in it revolves, the hour pointing to the fixed roman quarter hour markers above. Here, the clock is saying 35 minutes past 2. (H082)*

makers of their day and neighbours in Fleet Street, exemplify the Golden Age's finest traditions. It is no surprise then that Lord Harris includes three genuine clocks by Tompion in his collection and no less than ten genuine examples by Knibb, any one of which would be a lifetime's ambition for a collector of more modest means.

The work of Joseph Knibb has been described as "the female of the species" and

Fig. 7. *8 day, roman striking, longcase clock with skeletonised chapter ring, in parquetry case by Joseph Knibb, c.1685. This is one of the rare clocks by Knibb with a case carcass made of cariniana wood rather than the more usual oak. (H092)*

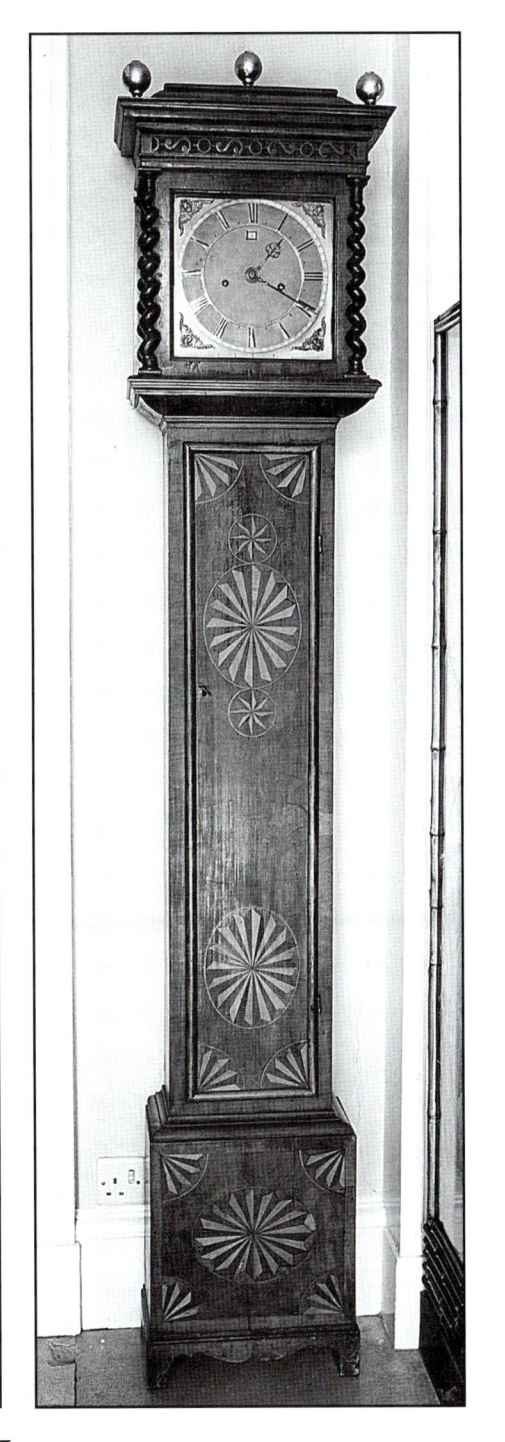

7

looking at the elegant styling of his clocks, *Plate 2* and *Fig. 7* one can see why. Thomas Tompion's work, *Fig. 8*, tended to be somewhat more solid, and masculine in feel, especially in the construction of the movement, though Knibb's was not necessarily less well made because of this fact.

In the early 1670s Joseph Knibb invented a number of refinements for his clockwork which became especially associated with him. Three of Belmont's Knibb clocks have roman striking, a system of striking the hours based on the roman notation on the dial. The system incorporates two bells, one high ('ding') and one low ('dong'). The high bell denotes a roman 'I' and the low bell a roman 'V'. The roman 'X' is denoted by two blows on the low bell. Thus six o'clock (VI) is struck 'dong-ding', and twelve o'clock (XII) is struck 'dong-dong, ding-ding'. Knibb appears to have invented the idea, about 1675, in order to reduce the driving force needed. In the weight-driven clocks this meant lighter driving weights which would enable Knibb to use a finer, more elegant case. These clocks of Knibb's always have a 'IV' for a four on the chapter ring of the dial, rather than the correct 'IIII', to indicate that the clock has this special form of striking.

Another invention of Knibb's, probably intended to improve timekeeping, was a new form of escapement known as the 'tic-tac'. In fact, the only clock in the collection to have Knibb's version of this escapement is one by Tompion, *Fig. 9*. Indeed, there is evidence to suggest that

Fig. 8. *8 day longcase clock No. 227 in walnut case by Thomas Tompion, c.1695. This and the Knibb in* Fig. 7 *have always been in the entrance hall at Belmont; two great names encapsulating Lord Harris's collection. (H126)*

8

there was considerable exchange of ideas, and even of workmen and finished clockwork, between the two great workshops.

Daniel Quare (c.1647-1724) a contemporary of Tompion and Knibb, was another fine maker, a confirmed Quaker who was unable to take up the post of Royal Clockmaker because he refused to take the oath of allegiance. Four clocks typify his output, from a very ordinary but good quality lantern clock to the magnificent marquetry cased longcase clock, *Fig. 10,* made c.1715, with grande sonnerie striking: quarter striking with the

Fig. 9. *Small ebony-veneered, hour striking, 8 day spring clock, with tic-tac escapement, c.1680, by Thomas Tompion. (H128)*

Fig. 10. *Month going, grande sonnerie striking longcase clock No.145 by Daniel Quare, c.1715. The seaweed marquetry veneers on the case are exceptionally fine and extensive. This clock is of Quare's finest quality and might well have had a royal or aristocratic provenance. (H117)*

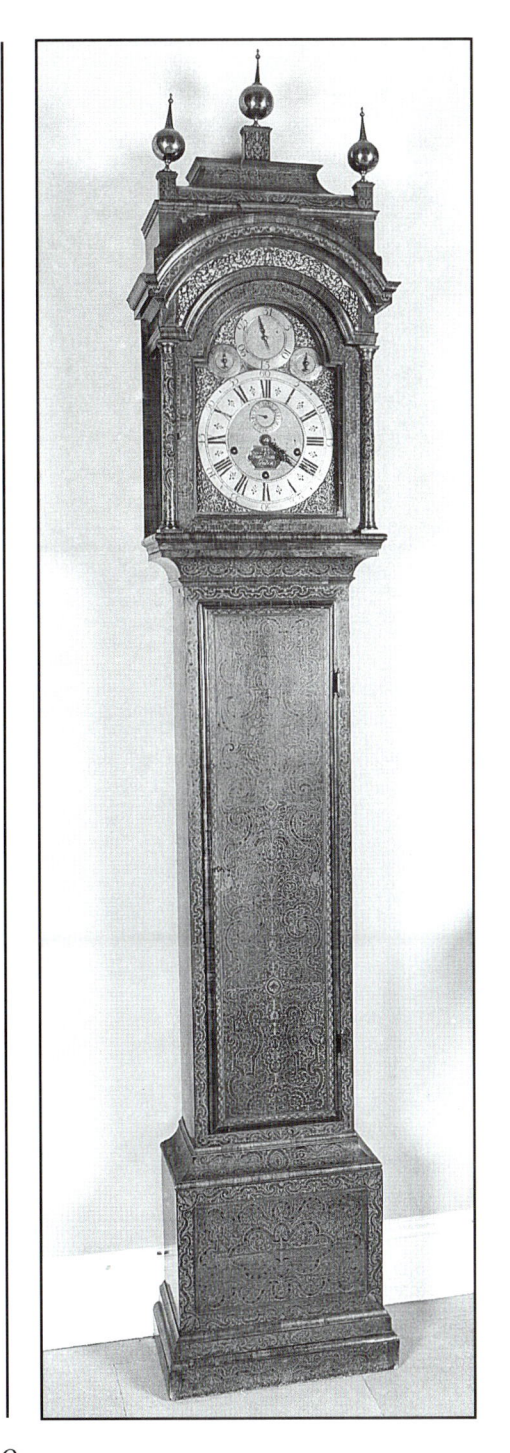

Fig. 11. *Gold cased watch by Edward Cockey. The outer, protective, case of the 'pair case' has* repoussé *decoration, hammered out from within, seen here on the open bezel of the outer case. The watch has a gold* champlevé *dial; literally 'raised fields' in the metal, upon which the numerals are engraved. (H306)*

previous hour repeated after each quarter. This is one of the clocks Harris acquired from Walter Iden.

Clock making in France at the turn of the seventeenth century is represented by two clocks in the collection, a quarter-striking longcase clock, c.1700, (with a number of later alterations to the case) by the great Parisian maker Pierre Gaudron (Master 1695, died 1745) and a very fine *tête-de-poupée* mantel clock, c.1680, *Plate 3*, by Claude Monnier of Paris (fl.1680-1700), the case almost certainly by the most famous of all French *ébénistes* (furniture makers) André Charles Boulle of Paris (1642-1732) who gave his name to the form of veneering on this case: *boullework*.

The Harris collection has a small number of interesting English watches, including a very fine clock-watch, a pocket watch which strikes the hours on a bell, by Falkiner of London c.1720, and a gold cased watch by Edward Cockey of Warminster, c.1726, *Fig. 11*, the case with symmetrical *repoussé* (hammered out) decoration.

The successor to Tompion's business was the equally talented if rather less flamboyant character of George Graham (c.1673-1751) who, from 1711, had been Tompion's assistant and had married his niece. Lord Harris greatly admired the man known, even in his own time, as "honest" George Graham, and there are four examples of his work, one longcase clock in an ebonised fruitwood and oak case and three spring clocks, one each of the three sizes Graham made. The largest, No. 488, *Fig. 12*, is grande sonnerie striking with a plain backplate to the movement, and the medium size, *Plate 2*, No. 596, and the smallest, *Fig. 13*, No. 608, have beautiful, profusely engraved backplates.

10

Precision Clocks of the late 18th century. The Golden Age may nominally end with Graham's death in 1751, but naturally London clock and watchmakers continued to make fine products. In this Age of Reason, a time of increasing scientific discovery and world exploration, work concentrated on improving precision timekeepers. The great John Harrison had shown in the early 1760s that a marine timekeeper was a practical possibility for improving global navigation and increasing numbers of precision timekeepers and 'regulators' (pendulum clocks specifically designed to

Fig. 14. *The hood and dial of the mahogany cased regulator by William Coombe, 1781. The lower dial is for seconds, the upper left for minutes and the right for hours.* (H034)

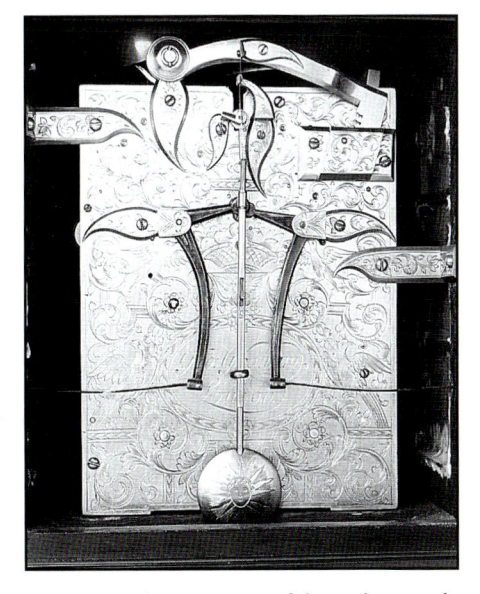

Fig. 13. *The movement of the striking and pull quarter repeating spring clock No. 608 by George Graham, c.1720. The profusely engraved backplate is typical for Graham's spring clocks.* (H071)

Fig. 12. *8 day grande sonnerie striking spring clock No. 488, in ebony veneered case, by George Graham, c.1715. The dials at the top are for regulation and for silencing the striking.* (H069)

keep accurate time) were being made, particularly for scientific functions like astronomy and navigation.

In the collection are precision clocks by, amongst others, Daniel Delander (1678-1733), John Ellicott (1706-1772) and George Margetts (1748-1804). The latter two would certainly have been used as serious astronomical regulators when first made, though for which Observatories will probably never now be known. The regulator by William Coombe of London on the other hand, *Fig. 14*, is well documented. It was commissioned from Coombe in 1781 by the Astronomer Royal, Nevil Maskelyne, with the intention of testing it at Greenwich and then sending it to the Grand Duke of Tuscany who was then equipping a new observatory in

11

Plate 2. *The Golden Age personified: (left to right) Spring clocks by George Graham, c.1720 (H070); Edward East c.1675 from Walter Iden's collection (H052); and Joseph Knibb, c.1680 (H089).*
The Knibb is month going and has the maker's roman striking system.

Florence to be known as 'La Specola'. Unfortunately, the regulator did not perform well and Maskelyne, who had already paid Coombe for it, decided to keep it for himself and had another made for the Duke by Larcum Kendall. The Coombe was bought by Harris, via a saleroom and a dealer, from the descendants of Maskelyne's family.

Towards the end of the eighteenth century, trade in decorative clocks to the Ottoman Empire, which had been a regular source of

Fig. 15. *Large, turkish market musical table clock by George Prior, c.1790 in* vernis martin *decorated case with crystal twist columns to the sides. The white enamel dial is marked with Islamic numerals as was usual on such clocks. (H112)*

income for London clockmakers for over a century, began to increase and, with a rapidly developing trade in clocks for India and the far East, some London clock and watchmakers now concentrated almost exclusively in these specialities. Timothy Williamson was one such and his clock c.1785 and watch c.1790, *Plate 4* and *rear cover*, are typical products for the Chinese market. George Prior, on the other hand, specialised in clocks for the Ottoman (Turkish) market and the clock by him, *Fig. 15*, is a good example. Grand as it is, it would originally have been grander still having a large cupola on top, probably with columns of crystal and gilt brass.

studied his collection. Watch No. 1416 by Breguet, *Plate 6*, is the finest at Belmont. According to the Breguet archive, still extant in Paris, this watch was made in 1812 for Antonio de Bourbon, one of the Spanish princes, for 6,000 francs. It has a full calendar, equation of time indication (the hand with the gold sun is the apparent

Plate 3. *A French Miscellany: (left to right) Lyre clock with the movement housed in the gridiron pendulum, by Lepaute of Paris c.1820 (H194); singing bird automaton, French made but retailed by Hurt and Wray of Birmingham c.1880 (H154); and a fine tête de poupée ('dolls head') clock by Monnier of Paris, c.1680. (H198)*

Revolutionary Horology.

If France can be considered as having an horological 'heyday' it would have to be around the revolutionary years, nominally between 1780 and 1820. During this time the French were unrivalled in both the technical and aesthetic elegance of their clock and watch designs. Abraham Louis Breguet (1748-1823) is arguably the most famous French horologist of all and was one of Lord Harris's particular favourites. George Graham and Breguet were the only two makers of whom Harris acquired engraved portraits and both hung in his workroom where he dismantled and

solar time hand) and lever escapement. The decidedly modern looking watch No. 4517 by Breguet was made between 1825 and 1832 and has a detailed record of its manufacture supplied by Breguet to Lord Harris. It was sold to the Prince Demidoff for 4000 francs on 20 September 1836.

Five of the twenty three genuine watches by Breguet have his 'secret signature', *Fig. 16*, a tiny scribed name and number which was his means of distinguishing the genuine product. On the enamel dials this was below the XII and on the silver dials it was either side of it. The elegant little mantel clock by Breguet No. 1273, *Fig. 17*, was made for his friend Madame d'Eymar in 1804.

Figures 18 and *19* show a gold-cased watch of quality and elegance equal to Breguet's but which is in fact by LeRoy of Paris c.1800. It is of exceptional interest because it is an early example of a 'self winding' watch, known as a *perpetuelle*,

Fig. 16. *A.L.Breguet's secret signature on the white enamel dial of watch No. 230. The watch is in a gold case and has repeating for hours and ten minutes and, most unusually, for the date. It was made, c.1800, for M.Tallyrand. (H281)*

Fig. 17. *Mantel clock in mahogany case by Breguet, No. 1273, c.1804. The 'jump' hour hand advances in a sudden movement every half hour. (H174)*

14

Figs. 18 *and* 19. *Gold cased* perpetuelle *(self winding watch) by LeRoy of Paris, c.1800. The hands are of polished blued steel; the inner hand is for the day of the month. The lever across the back of the movement has a gold semicircular weight attached and it oscillates to and fro during daily use, winding the watch. (H318)*

another of Breguet's specialities. The escapement of the watch is also very rare; it is of the type known as the *virgule*, the 'comma' escapement. A related piece, in the Saloon at Belmont, signed simply 'Pierre LeRoy', and probably by the same maker, is the mahogany-cased regulator, with temperature-compensated gridiron pendulum, made c.1820. This also has a very rare form of escapement known as an *echappement a manivelle*, literally 'crank' escapement, with a little jewelled roller running in a slot in an extension to the crutch of the pendulum. The dial has an equation of time indication below the XII and the associated annual calendar below the VI, *Fig. 20*. The two winding holes are for two driving weights which run in a cavity in the back of the case. The clock does not strike and both weights drive the timekeeping part of the clock. Another French clock of the period is the lyre clock, *Plate 3*, made by Lepaute of Paris. Its movement is actually mounted within the bob of the gridiron pendulum and swings with it, adding a slightly mysterious air to what is already an intriguing and high quality clock.

One of the four pieces by Antide Janvier (1751-1835) at Belmont is seen in *Fig. 21*. Janvier was much less of a businessman than Breguet and his production was considerably smaller, but his bold and

Fig. 21. *Complex mantel regulator by Antide Janvier, No. 999, c.1820. The dials include times of sunrise and sunset, the equation of time and the lunar calendar. (H189)*

15

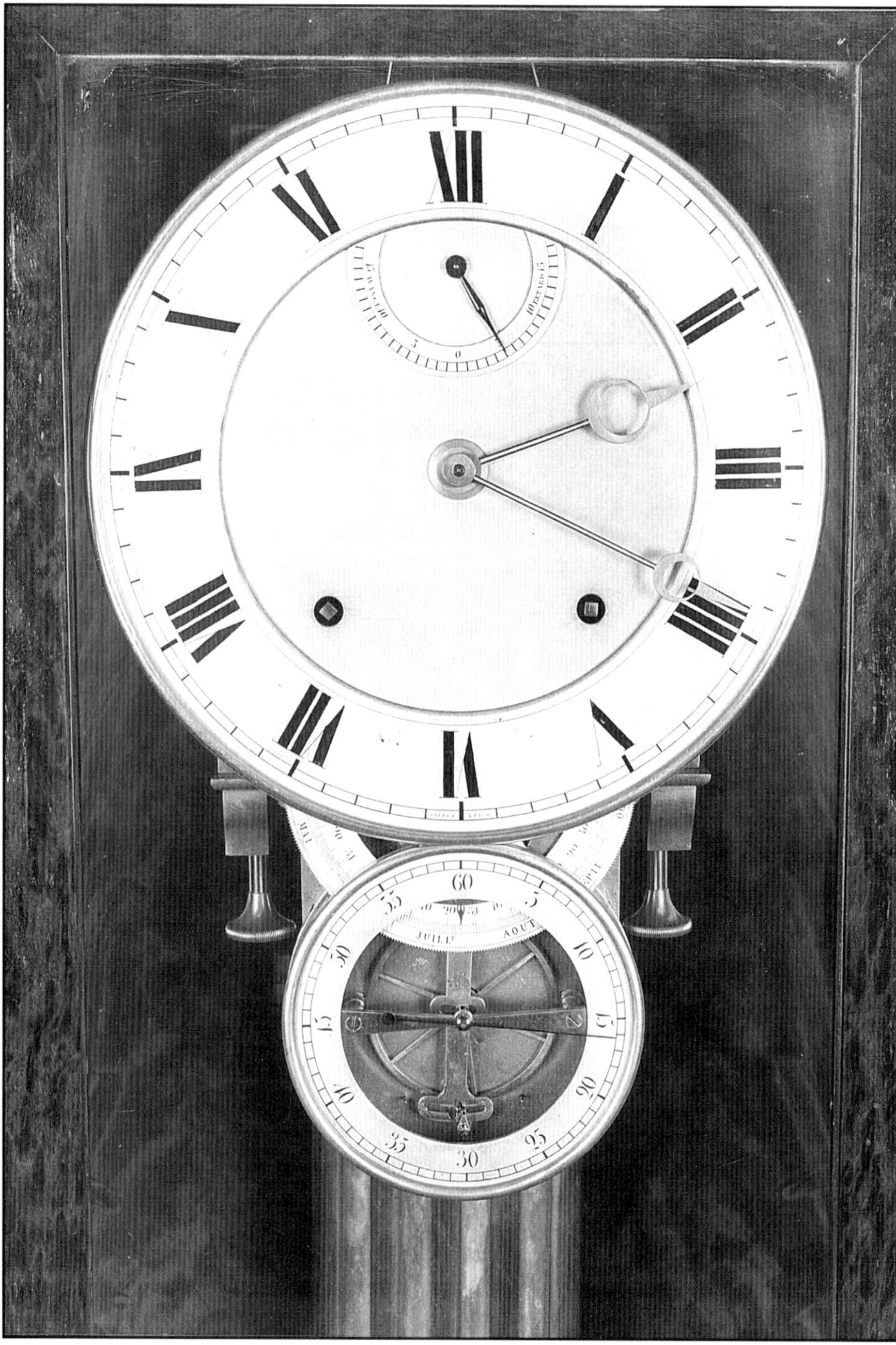

stylish designs have always made him a favourite with the horological cognoscente. It was Janvier who first designed the most famous version of the orrery clock, *front cover*, a design made in some numbers by Raingo Freres in Paris during the 1820s and 30s. This clock is signed Raingo, Paris, and dates from c.1830. The orrery is the instrument mounted on top of the clock and, driven round by it, represents the solar system in motion. In these clocks the orrery only includes the Sun (at the centre), the Earth and the Moon, but both Earth and Moon move at their correct rates and are in their correct positions at all times, the whole assembly rotating one revolution in a year.

Intended as both an opulent furnishing piece for the wealthy and, to some extent as an educational toy, the orrery can be disconnected from the clock and driven round quickly for demonstration by turning a little ivory handle on the side. They say 'one has to entertain before one can educate' and these clocks often incorporate a musical box in the base. This one has a slightly later replacement mechanism playing airs from the opera *Der Freischutz*, by Weber.

Fig. 20. *The dial of the regulator by LeRoy. The lower dial is for seconds and has the escapement visible within it. The equation of time, the difference between solar (sun) time and mean (clock) time is indicated by the dial below the XII. (H197)*

Fig. 22. *Wagon spring shelf clock by Birge and Fuller of Bristol, Connecticut, c.1845. Unlike the later American shelf clocks, this type was not exported to Britain and is particularly rare over here.*
The movement is driven by a 'wagon' (leaf) spring housed in the base of the clock; the design was patented by its inventor, Joseph Ives, in 1845. (H228)

Victorian Masterpieces. With the 19th century came the era of mass production. The Americans were the first to set up manufacturing of products with truly interchangeable parts, first in the firearms industry and then in clock making manufactories in the mid-1840s. Since the early years of the century they had been organising clockmaking on a much more production-orientated footing and two clocks at Belmont are from this time. The rare, 8 day, wagon spring clock, *Fig. 22*, made by Birge and Fuller of Bristol, Connecticut, c.1845, is driven by a heavy steel leaf spring in the base. This design of clock arose from the Americans' inability at that time to make or buy inexpensive steel clock springs. Another, slightly later, 8 day clock by Brewster and Ingrahams in the

17

Fig. 23. *Marine chronometer by Thomas Earnshaw, No. 811. The movement is contained in a mahogany box with typical brass gimbals to ensure the movement remains horizontal even if the box tilts. (H253)*

collection actually has brass mainsprings for the same reason and, most unusually, is hour-repeating, having rack striking. The French by this time were also making clocks by methods more akin to mass production, but of a relatively high quality, and both the Americans and the French now exported into Europe and particularly Britain. The result was that the English clockmaking trade was forced to specialise in the highest quality sector only, and for a category of customer whose numbers were diminishing every year. It was the

beginning of the end for the English clockmaking tradition, but the period did see the making of some exceedingly fine specialist articles. The best of those essential navigational aids, marine and pocket chronometers, could still only be bought from London makers and the Harris collection includes examples by the best of them. The marine chronometer No. 811 by the pioneering chronometer maker Thomas Earnshaw (1749-1829), c.1800, *Fig. 23*, has an entirely original movement, although the box is a mid 19th century replacement, something which happened very often with these functional timekeepers.

The pocket chronometer by Arnold and Dent No. 5413 is notable because it was: "Presented by H.R.H. Prince Albert to Comdr. William Allen of HMS Wilberforce on his departure with the expedition to the Niger for the abolition of the slave trade 25th March 1841". Edward J. Dents' (1790-1853) productions typify the high quality precision work of Victorian clock and watchmakers. There are six objects by this maker at Belmont. *Fig. 24* is a quarter striking, precision carriage clock by Dent, a large clock in every sense, standing 18 inches high and weighing in at over 56 lbs! Another fine clock by Dent is the mantel regulator, No. 508, c.1840, with a detached detent escapement designed by the Astronomer Royal, George Biddell Airy. Just as Tompion and Graham had before him, Dent formed a close business relationship with the Royal Observatory at Greenwich, making many of their regulators and other timekeeping devices, and gaining huge prestige and many valuable commissions from elsewhere as a result.

Dent was not, however, Royal Clockmaker. This title had remained with the Vulliamy family of clockmakers since the 18th

18

century and the formidable and influential Benjamin Lewis Vulliamy (1780-1854), one of Dent's great rivals, held the post. The exceptionally high grade clocks made by the Vulliamys are represented by six objects: a silver-mounted spring clock by the first of the dynasty, Justin Vulliamy (nothing by his son Benjamin) and then three mantel clocks and two regulators by Benjamin's son, Benjamin Lewis. It is difficult to imagine how one could improve on the quality of the regulators, made as a pair in 1849 (H135 and H136) being admired by Lord Harris in *Fig. 1*. The aesthetics of their case design may not be to everyone's taste - Lady Harris referred to them disparagingly as "the petrol pumps" - but the massively solid brass movements, with their jewelled dead beat escapements and a host of fine detail, are guaranteed to receive gasps of admiration when the hoods come off. The Amboyna-veneered cases are impressive too, veneered inside and out, and with patent hinges and (Bramah) locks, these clocks must have been made for a very special, and presumably an exceedingly wealthy, customer. Lord Harris actually first acquired just one of these clocks, not knowing that there was originally a pair to it. It was only by coincidence, when he visited his friend and fellow collector Cecil Clutton one day, that he saw the other clock. Remembering that his was marked 'Sidereal Time' and seeing Clutton's was 'Mean Time', and that they had consecutive serial numbers, he realised they had been a pair and immediately negotiated with Clutton to reunite them.

While considering clocks of High Victorian origin, mention must be made of the little 'collection within a collection'. This is the fifteen clocks by, or in imitation of, Thomas Cole (1800-1864), a maker whose products achieved major fashion status during Victoria's reign. Reflecting

Fig. 24. Large gilt brass precision carriage clock by Dent, c.1880. The fusee movement has a dead beat escapement, mercurial compensation pendulum and Harrison's maintaining power. The clock is also quarter striking on four bells and one large gong. (H043)

the contemporary fondness for looking back and reviving earlier styles, Cole's clocks were usually housed in heavily engraved gilt brass cases, reminiscent of German renaissance table clocks, but alloyed with wholly new and idiosyncratic designs for dials and forms of case. *Fig. 25* is the probably unique model incorporated in a cake dish with a concave dial, concave hands and a concave glass. There are several other off-beat examples at Belmont, including an exceptional, large, floor standing clock with seconds pendulum, single beat escapement and time, calendar and lunar dials disposed on three sides.

The ultimate in Victorian watchmaking is personified by the gold-cased pocket watch No. 09182/11487, *Plate 5*, by Charles Frodsham (1810-1871), another of Dent's rivals. This has a lever escapement tourbillon movement by the top watchmakers of the day, Nicole Nielsen, and is the 'state of the art' high-precision pocket watch of its time. Watches such as this, made for wealthy civil customers rather than the Navy (this watch was made for the Marquis of Bath), were usually tested at Kew Observatory (later the

Plate 4. *Quarter striking, centre seconds calendar watch by Timothy Williamson c.1790. A typically complex watch for the Chinese export market. (H331)*

Plate 5. *Three fine watches: (left to right) Gold cased tourbillon watch No. 09182/ 11487 by Frodsham, 1907 (H313); gold watch No. 1416 by Breguet (H285), the property of horologist Malcolm Webster (son of Percy Webster); gold watch No. 4517 with equation of time and calendar indications by Breguet, an unusually slim design for an equation watch. (H299)*

20

Fig. 26. *Automaton picture clock, c.1845. A separate mechanism in the back of the picture provides the music and the automation to the figures. The elaborate frame is of wood and gilt gesso. (H150)*

Fig. 25. *Gilt metal table clock in the form of a cake dish, in the manner of Thomas Cole, retailed by Jenner and Newstub, c.1870. (H032)*

National Physical Laboratory) rather than at Greenwich. In trials at Kew this particular timekeeper was awarded the highest marks of any English watch ever tested at the Observatory, with an astonishing 93.9 marks out of 100.

21

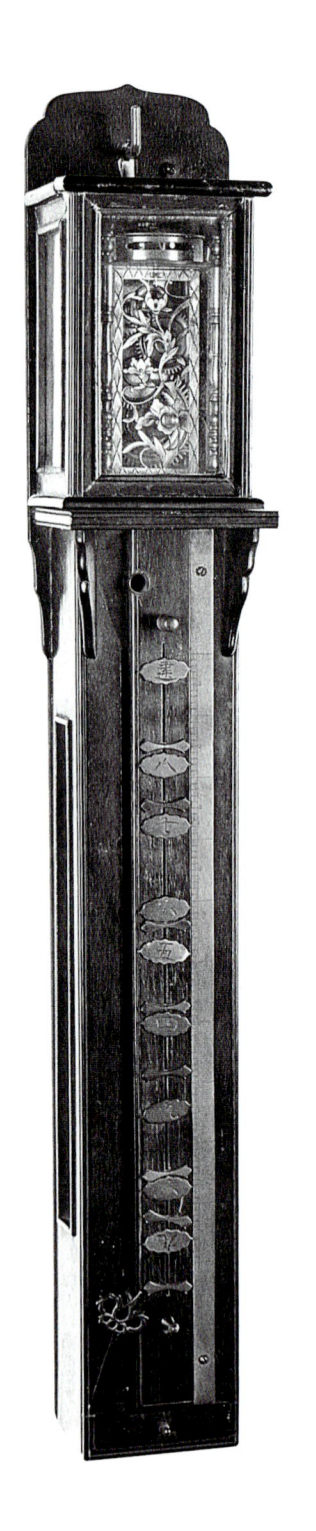

Mysteries and Novelties. Lord Harris was in fact rather a shy, retiring character, but he certainly had a sense of humour too. The automata pictures in the collection, such as the French barber's shop scene, c.1845, *Fig. 26*, in which the monkeys spring to life, nodding and gesticulating in time to a jolly tune at every hour, are just plain good fun. The French singing bird automata, c.1880, *Plate 3*, is another splendid example with birds chattering and whistling away as they hop from branch to branch and drink from the 'stream' (created by rotating twisted glass rods) in the most lifelike way.

Some clocks are, in a sense, mysterious purely because they come from a culture remote from our own. Such is the case with the four Japanese clocks, all of which indicate the time in temporal hours, with moveable hour markers to enable the periods of daylight and darkness always to contain six 'hours' each. *Fig. 27* shows the Japanese pillar clock with its markers down the centre, the time being indicated by the descending pointer shown at the bottom of the scale. The markers had to be rearranged every two weeks or so, to ensure they kept in step with the seasons!

Perhaps the clock horologists think of first when the title 'mystery clock' is mentioned is that devised by Robert Houdin of Paris, c.1830, one of which is at Belmont. This type has a see-through glass dial, with the numerals painted on it, and an apparently unconnected single hour hand mounted in the centre; but the hand moves and tells the time. How does it do it? In fact there are *two* sheets of glass, one static with the

Fig. 27. *Mid 19th century Japanese pillar clock. Winding the clock up at dusk raises the pointer and its descent over 24 hours, past the 12 'hour' markers of night and day, indicates the time. (H239)*

Fig. 28. Reproduction 'Mysterious circulator' clock, by Dent of London, 1972. The tail of the hand, here partially obscured by the dolphin support, contains the movement with its eccentric weight. (H048)

numerals on it, the other, with the hand attached, having a thin brass toothed edge hidden in the rim of the dial. This is driven by a tiny endless screw which in turn is driven from the movement in the base via a series of thin jointed shafts running up inside the structure.

Another example is the 'mysterious circulator' clock, *Fig. 28*, which really does have a hand unconnected with any remote driving mechanism, and yet that hand also moves and tells the time, pointing to the dial surrounding it. If the hand is pushed it will spin freely round and round, but will always come back to telling the right time. This clever design was apparently thought up by a German inventor about 1800 and its secret lies in the tail of the hand which contains a small watch movement. The hand is carefully balanced but the movement has a small eccentric weight added to where the movement's little 'hour hand' would have been. As the weight turns in the course of 12 hours, so it unbalances the hand and causes it to turn steadily within the main dial band. With the weight fully away from the centre of the dial the hand is 'tail-heavy' and points to XII. In six hours' time the weight will have moved round to be closest to the centre of the dial and the hand has, in the course of the six hours, moved steadily round to point to VI. Belmont's mysterious circulator is a reproduction by Dent, made in 1972.

Fig. 29. Reproduction inclined plane clock by Dent, 1970. The dial is eccentrically weighted to ensure that it always remains vertical as the drum gradually descends the slope. (H044)

Fig. 30. *Reproduction rolling ball clock by Thwaites and Reed, London 1972. As it traverses the zig-zag track, taking one second for each traverse, the ball passes under a bridge marked with seconds. It takes fifteen seconds to reach the end of the track. (H033)*

Dent also made the reproduction mystery clock known as the inclined plane clock, *Fig. 29*, made in 1970 but which is an idea dating from renaissance Germany. The clock in the drum sits on the slope but does not immediately roll down. In fact it *is* rolling down, but very slowly. Inside there is a heavy eccentric weight attached to the movement and dial, but this assembly is in geared contact only with the inside of the drum. As the drum and movement/weight together try to roll down the slope the weight, being eccentric within the drum, has to rise up on one side and the drum cannot continue to roll. However, in trying to roll down, the eccentric weight and movement inside the drum press against the drum's toothed rim, which causes the movement to be driven. With the movement ticking, the drum is able, very slowly, to descend the slope. In the course of one week the drum will have reached the bottom, passing by the days of the week engraved on the side of the slope as it goes. To 'wind it up' one only has to pick up the drum and place it at the top of the slope again!

The most well known in this 'novelty' category of Harris's clocks has to be the reproduction rolling ball clock, made by Thwaites and Reed in 1972, after William Congreve's design patented in 1808, *Fig. 30*. What is perhaps not so well known is that Congreve, 'Superintendent